JOURNEY THROUGH *the*
CREATION MUSEUM

PREPARE TO BELIEVE

First printing: September 2008

ISBN-13: 978-0-89051-530-3
ISBN-10: 0-89051-530-1

Library of Congress Number: 2008935150

All scripture quotations are taken from the
New King James Version

Cover design by Left Coast Design, Inc.
Interior design by Diana Bogardus & Rebekah Krall

Printed in U.S.A.

Please visit our web site for other great titles:
www.masterbooks.net

For information regarding author interviews, please contact
the publicity department at (870) 438-5288

JOURNEY THROUGH *the*
CREATION MUSEUM

PREPARE TO BELIEVE

As people visit the Answers in Genesis (AiG) Creation Museum, I am overwhelmed by the positive responses. People say how grateful and thankful they are that such a God-honoring place so boldly standing on the authority of God's Word, defending the Christian faith and proclaiming the gospel exists in this very secularized culture.

However, this is not just AiG's Museum — it is your museum. God's people from every walk of life and all ages contributed to this place either financially, through prayer, volunteer help or in a myriad of other ways.

What happened here at the Creation Museum is a 'God thing.' We often said it was a 'God-sized project.' It is a miracle of existence. AiG certainly organized the construction and exhibit design, but this place is for everyone. It is for you to use so that Christians will be equipped and non-Christians challenged concerning the truth of God's Word, and the gospel of Jesus Christ.

As you look through these pages, please don't marvel at what people have been able to build, but marvel at what God has accomplished through His dedicated people.

— Ken Ham

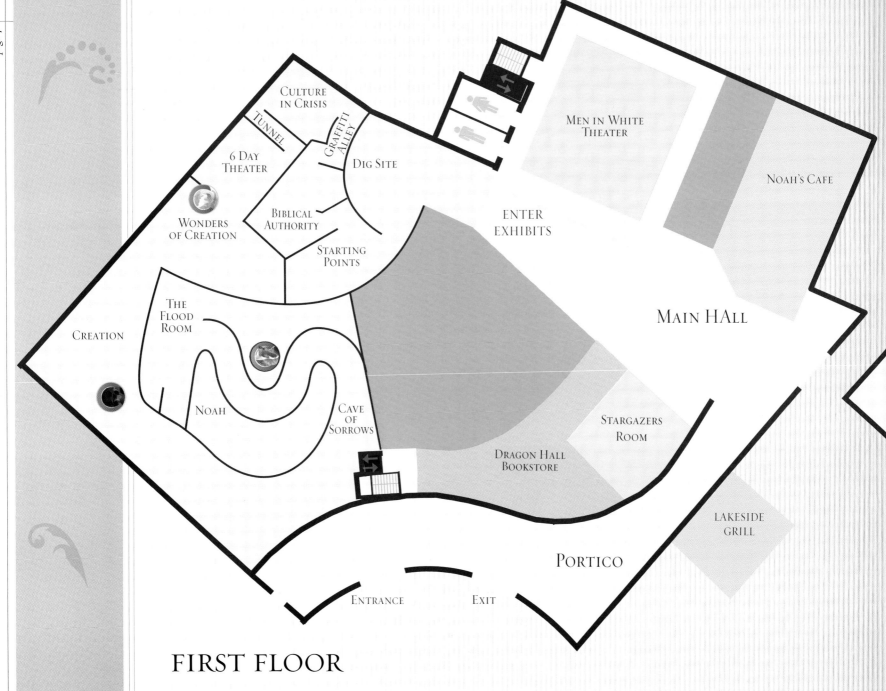

CULTURE
in CRISIS

TUNNEL

GRAFFITI ALLEY

6 DAY
THEATER

DIG SITE

WONDERS
of CREATION

BIBLICAL
AUTHORITY

STARTING
POINTS

MEN in WHITE
THEATER

NOAH'S CAFE

ENTER
EXHIBITS

CREATION

THE
FLOOD
ROOM

MAIN HALL

NOAH

CAVE
OF
SORROWS

STARGAZERS
ROOM

DRAGON HALL
BOOKSTORE

LAKESIDE
GRILL

PORTICO

ENTRANCE   EXIT

FIRST FLOOR

SECOND FLOOR

Flood Geology Room

Babel Confusion

3 C's Room

Chapel

Last Adam Theater

Palm Plaza

Dinosaur Den

Dragon Theater

Palm Cafe

Morris Whitcomb Lecture Rooms

Discovery Hall

TABLE OF CONTENTS

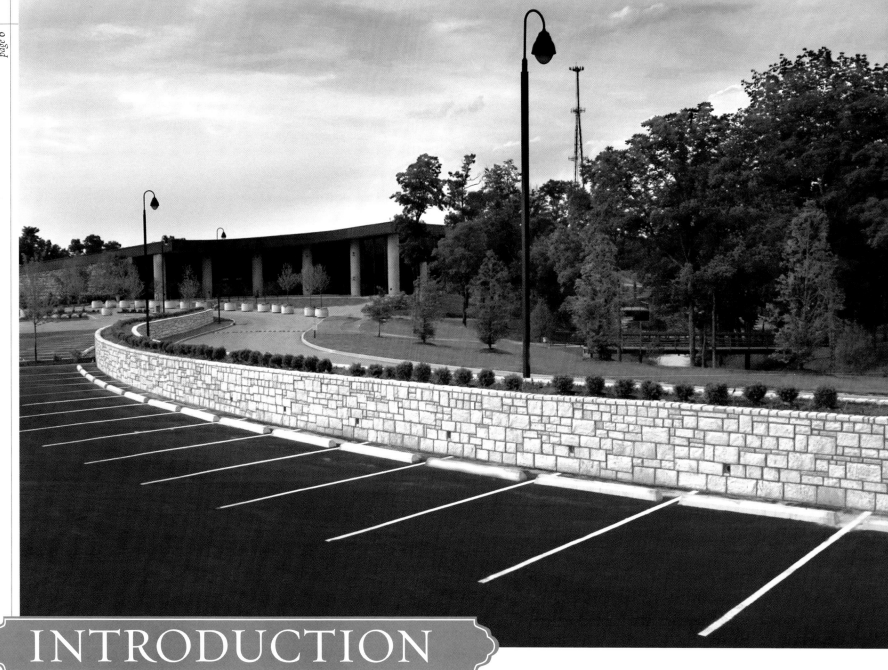

INTRODUCTION

The vision for the Creation Museum is something that percolated in my heart for over 30 years before it came to pass. As a public school science teacher in Australia in the 1970's, I took my students on excursions to science museums. I was burdened when I saw them being exposed to evolution and millions of years as fact. Evolution and millions of years was a stumbling block to the students considering the claims of the gospel, because they thought the Bible could not be true.

While visiting one secular museum, I heard a father say to his young son as they stood in front of the "ape-man" exhibit, "This was your ancestor." My heart ached. I also found out that most people in our local churches in Australia thought you had to believe in evolution and millions of years. As a result, my cry to the Lord was: "Why can't we have a creation museum that teaches the truth?" That was over 30 years ago, but the burden only intensified year after year.

Because of a father and mother who stood on the authority of the Word of God, who would not knowingly compromise biblical truths, and who taught their children to defend the Christian faith and actively stand up for the accuracy of God's Word, the Lord used that foundation in my life to put a "fire shut up in my bones," as Jeremiah described it (Jer. 20:9). I wanted to see a ministry that would combat the lie of evolution and call the church and culture back to the authority of the Word of God.

I really had no option. The Lord grabbed hold of me and burdened me so intensely concerning this message about biblical authority and the gospel. He has given me a real zeal and stamina I cannot explain from a human perspective.

Unfortunately, we had no idea how to build a creation museum or design its exhibits. However, because the burden to build this was so great, we stepped out in faith, not willing to give up even when it seemed everything was against us, such as the time we lost our first piece of property because of the opposition from a humanist group.

But God did something far greater than we could have ever imagined. He provided a superior piece of property and brought people to the ministry (like exhibit designer Patrick Marsh and hundreds of others) who we never even dreamed possible to be part of this huge project. God provided the people and resources to take this vision to levels higher than we could have ever imagined. Now, would the donations be provided? Would people come? We pressed on, and all I can say now is, "Look what God has done!"

That burden, that "fire shut up in my bones," is still being intensified. When one secular reporter asked me at the opening of the museum, "Do you have any plans for the future, or is this it?" I answered, "You haven't seen anything yet!" I believe the Lord has much more in store for this ministry. As Noah's ark stood as a warning to the world of impending judgment, yet it pictured salvation with the door open, so I believe God is using this ministry as He did with Noah: to warn the world of coming judgment while offering God's free gift of salvation through an open door.

Journey with us through this museum that is being used by God to change hearts and minds. May it put a "fire" in the bones of you and your children to proclaim the truth and authority of God's Word.

Ken Ham

Ken Ham
President of Answers in Genesis

"In the beginning
God created the
heavens and
the earth."
—GENESIS 1:1

7 C's in God's Eternal Plan

Seven pivotal events from the beginning to the end of time

Creation

In the beginning—in six, 24-hour days—God made a perfect *creation*.

Corruption

The first man, Adam, disobeyed the Creator. His sin brought death and *corruption* into the creation.

Catastrophe

Adam's race became so wicked that God judged the earth with a great *catastrophe*—a global Flood—saving only those on the ark built by Noah.

Confusion

When Noah's descendents disobeyed God's command to fill the earth, God brought *confusion* on their language, forcing them to spread over the earth.

Christ

The Creator became a man, Jesus *Christ*, who obeyed God in everything, unlike the first man, Adam.

Cross

Jesus, the Messiah, died on a *cross* to pay the penalty for mankind's sin against God. He rose from the dead, providing life for all who trust in Him.

Consummation

One day, at the *consummation*, the Creator will remake His creation. He will cast out death and the disobedient, and dwell eternally with those who trust in Him.

But sanctify the Lord God in your hearts,
and always be ready to give a defense to
everyone who asks you a reason for the hope
that is in you, with meekness and fear;
— I PETER 3:15

THE MAIN HALL

From the first steps into the Creation Museum, it is clear this will be a remarkable experience! When visitors walk into the main hall, they are amazed by the animatronic dinosaurs and children, the waterfall, the towering trees, large aquarium, and live animal exhibits.

Did you notice the animatronic children have middle brown color skin? As people find out later in the museum's Babel exhibit, all humans have one basic skin color and Adam and Eve probably started out as middle brown.

The 40-ft long animatronic sauropod captivates everybody's attention as it moves, swinging its long neck slowly to the side.

The turtles look so real, but these turtles were sculpted by talented artists, helping people understand the complexity of the world God created.

LIVE ANIMAL EXHIBITS

Unique displays and live animal exhibits such as the colorful variety of finches, poison dart frogs, and the versatile chameleon not only fascinate people but teach important truths concerning the book of Genesis, and the creations of God which exist all around us.

WATERFALL EXHIBIT

Why are live gar fish swimming in the pool? (Hint-they are "living fossils.") Why are two baby animatronic *T. rex* dinosaurs standing beside two children at play? To challenge people right from the start of their museum experience about the coexistence of dinosaurs and people. This exhibit gets people thinking before they discover even more answers that await in the rest of the museum.

Then God made two great lights: the greater light to rule the day, and the lesser light to rule the night. He made the stars also. God set them in the firmament of the heavens to give light on the earth, and to rule over the day and over the night, and to divide the light from the darkness. And God saw that it was good.
—Genesis 1:16-18

STARGAZERS ROOM

PLANETARIUM

The Stargazer's Room features a Digistar 3 SP2 digital projection system — providing a full color, high-resolution environment that is truly awe-inspiring.

Sit back and be amazed as the projector displays vividly realistic cosmic images upon a 30-foot diameter hemispherical dome, allowing viewers to virtually travel anywhere in the universe. In the premier presentation "the Created Cosmos," visitors get to experience the incredible size of God's creation in an unforgettable journey.

The program takes us from the earth, to Orion's Belt, past several extra solar planets, into a globular star cluster, and then beyond the Milky Way to the extreme limit of the known universe. Viewers get a small taste of God's power as they experience the size of the universe in a way never before possible.

SHOW SELECTIONS

A number of different shows are played in the Stargazer's Room. In "The Created Cosmos," viewers are held spellbound as they begin to comprehend the size and complexity of the universe, and the awesome power of God. In "Worlds of Creation," viewers get to travel through the solar system and see how each of the planets exemplifies God's creative design. And for those who attend "The Christmas Star," viewers travel back in time to Bethlehem and examine events proclaiming the birth of the King of kings.

The state-of-the-art planetarium has seating for 78 people — a comfortable setting complete with specially-designed carpeting from Ireland.

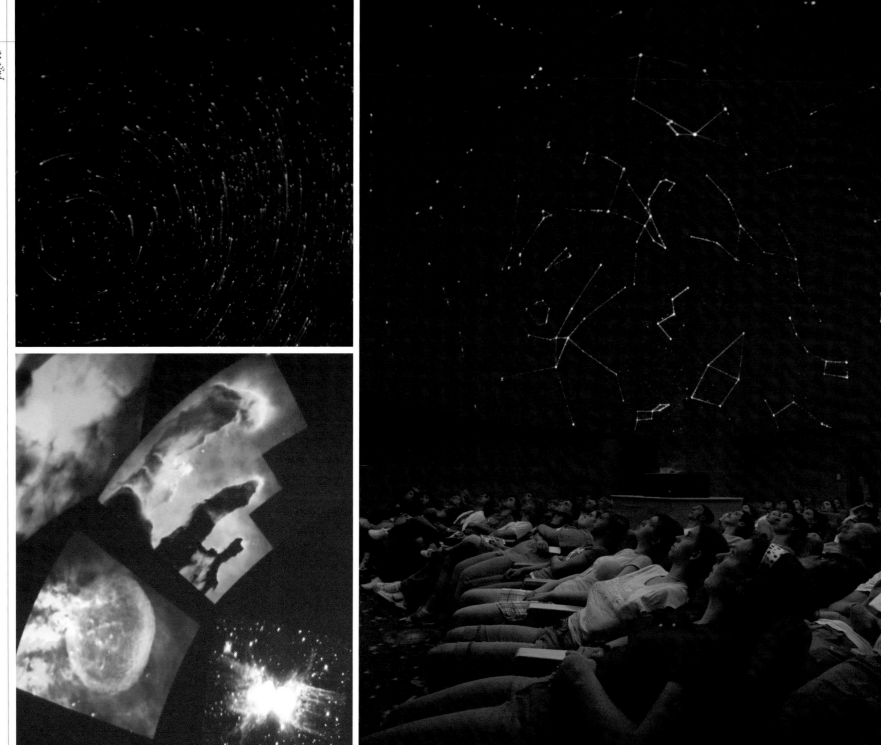

Astrophysicist Jason Lisle wrote and designed the breath-taking program for the planetarium, which show guests the great vastness and amazing design of God's creation.

Most importantly, the Stargazer's Room honors God in a way that very few planetariums do — by acknowledging the absolute authority of the Word of God beginning with Genesis. Like all the programs at the Creation Museum, the planetarium is firmly based on the Bible, and presents powerful information that challenges the secular worldview. The Stargazer's Room affirms what the Bible says in Psalm 19:1.

"The heavens declare the glory of God; And the firmament shows His handiwork."
—PSALM 19:1

MEN IN WHITE

MEN IN WHITE

Where a young girl has some very important questions of faith, two unforgettable (and very entertaining!) angels show up to give her vital biblical answers in this special production.

SPECIAL EFFECTS THEATER

Visitors to this high-tech auditorium will discover lots of surprises — vibrating seats, strobe lights, and sprays of water — all to create a memorable sensory experience as part of this uniquely presentation.

GRAND CANYON

Just past the waterfall and live animal exhibits is the entrance to the main part of the Creation Museum. A long time and a little bit of water or a lot of water and a little bit of time? — that is the question to ponder as you walk through the Grand Canyon to the Mount St. Helens ranger station.

DIG SITE

Two scientists, one a creationist, one an evolutionist with two different interpretations of the history of this dinosaur skeleton. Why?

WHY?

DIG SITE

The evidence is in the *Present*...

...but what happened in the *Past?*

COAL MINE: Were the vast coal beds around the globe formed slowly, over millions of years? Or are there other processes that can account for their formation in just thousands of years? Clues and evidence can be found in the geologic record and in fossils that are discovered — and this evidence supports the history of catastrophe and death detailed in the biblical book of Genesis.

FOSSILS: Millions of years old, or just thousands?

LUCY: Is Lucy really our ancestor? Or is she just a knuckle-dragging ape that spent most of her time in the trees? The true history of man is revealed in the Bible and shown in the Museum.

TRILOBITES: What caused the rapid burial of these trilobites, and of millions of other creatures around the world? Was it slow, gradual processes, or one large catastrophe? Guests learn the answer as they continue their walk through history.

Different Views of the Past

Same Plants and Animals

Same Apes and Humans

Same Rocks

Same Fossils

The pre

HUMAN REASON   GOD'S WORD

HUMAN REASON   GOD'S WORD

Human Reason   God's Word

STARTING POINTS

Same facts, but different views... *why?*

STARTING POINTS ROOM

Ultimately, to understand the origin of life and the universe, there are only two possible places to start: (a) the Word of the One Who has always been there and knows everything (the Creator God of the Bible) or (b) autonomous human reason (man's beliefs).

Based on these two starting points, there are different interpretations of the same evidence. The different starting points explain why the different views about origins are in conflict — because there are two totally different worldviews.

WHY?

Do different starting points matter in our personal lives?

Why am I here?   Am I alone?   Why do I suffer?   Is there any hope?   Why do we have to die?

DIFFERENT INTERPRETATIONS:

▶ The evolutionary scientist "sees" millions of years.

▶ The creation scientist "sees" thousands of years.

Two different interpretations because of two different starting points as demonstrated on the chart (next page, at right).

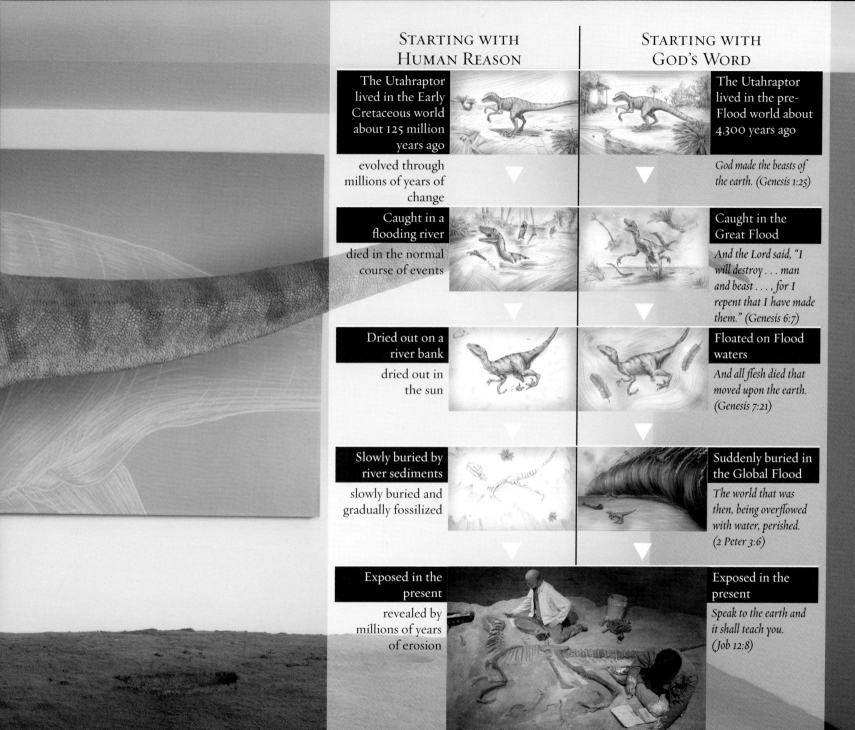

STARTING WITH HUMAN REASON	STARTING WITH GOD'S WORD
The Utahraptor lived in the Early Cretaceous world about 125 million years ago	The Utahraptor lived in the pre-Flood world about 4,300 years ago
evolved through millions of years of change	*God made the beasts of the earth. (Genesis 1:25)*
Caught in a flooding river	Caught in the Great Flood
died in the normal course of events	*And the Lord said, "I will destroy . . . man and beast . . . , for I repent that I have made them." (Genesis 6:7)*
Dried out on a river bank	Floated on Flood waters
dried out in the sun	*And all flesh died that moved upon the earth. (Genesis 7:21)*
Slowly buried by river sediments	Suddenly buried in the Global Flood
slowly buried and gradually fossilized	*The world that was then, being overflowed with water, perished. (2 Peter 3:6)*
Exposed in the present	Exposed in the present
revealed by millions of years of erosion	*Speak to the earth and it shall teach you. (Job 12:8)*

...eatly **Confirmed** that the Bible's HISTORICAL DETAILS are acc...

...the ORIGINAL WORDS have been...

reds of BIBLE PROPHECIES have been fulfilled, and **none has failed.**

ABOVE ALL, the GOD of TRUTH, the CREATOR of heaven and earth, inspired the men who penned the words.

BIBLICAL AUTHORITY

MOSES

BIBLICAL AUTHORITY ROOM

At the Creation Museum, no apology is made about the fact that our starting point is the Bible. This Book is a written revelation from One who knows everything and who inspired His prophets and apostles to write down for mankind the true history of the world. Throughout the Creation Museum, observational science (biology, geology, etc.) is used to confirm that the Bible's history truly explains the world.

This room gives examples of witnesses down through the ages who attest to the truthfulness of God's Word.

DAVID

ISAIAH

PAUL

This sign on the far wall of the Biblical Authority Room illustrates how God's Word has been under attack since the temptation of Adam and Eve in the Garden of Eden. Today's teaching that history goes back millions of years is just the latest attack on the authority of God's Word, which says God created everything a few thousand years ago.

MARTIN LUTHER EXHIBIT

Throughout history, there have been movements to return to God's Word when it has been attacked. In the sixteenth century, Martin Luther began a movement called the Reformation, which called people back to the authority of the Word of God.

GUTTENBERG PRESS EXHIBIT

As part of the Reformation, God's Word was copied and distributed among believers and around the world. The invention of the Guttenberg Press enabled copies of God's Word to be distributed more widely than ever before.

SCOPES TRIAL EXHIBIT

The Scopes Trial in 1925 marked a turning point in American history. The world press saw that Christians and the church had compromised with the notion of millions of years, so Christians no longer had adequate answers to defend the Christian faith. This battle of creation vs. evolution in school began in a small town in Tennessee. Many families who believe the biblical account of Genesis seek Christian schools, or choose home school as education options.

Templeton Denies Faith

Famed Christian Evangelist Accepts Evolution Becomes Atheist Evangelist

Born in 1915, Charles Templeton was generally acknowledged to be the most versatile of the new young evangelists. Templeton soon rose to prominence, even surpassing another dynamic young preacher, Billy Graham. In 1946, he was ranked among those best used of God by the National Association of Evangelicals.

As the pastor of the rapidly growing Avenue Road Church in Toronto, which he started with only his family and a few friends, Templeton also became one of the vice presidents of the newly formed Youth For Christ organization in 1945. He nominated his good friend, Billy Graham, to be field evangelist for the new ministry. Templeton, Graham, and a few others regularly spoke to thousands, pointing many to Christ both in America and Europe.

Newspapers and magazines carried reports of his meetings informing readers he was winning 150 converts a night. In Evansville, Indiana, the total attendance for the two-week campaign was 91,000 in a population of 128,000. Church attendance went up 17%.

However, despite his popularity and growing success as an evangelist, all was not well with Charles Templeton. The more he read, the more he found he was troubled, the more he began to question the essentials of Christian faith because he could no longer believe God's Word beginning with Genesis.

In a chat with Billy Graham about Templeton's desire to attend Princeton Theological Seminary, Templeton stated: "But Billy, it's simply not possible any longer to believe, for instance, the biblical account of creation. The world was not created over a period of days a few thousand years ago; it has evolved over millions of years. It's not a matter of

like Charles Darwin, had a big problem understanding how one could reconcile an earth full of death, disease, and suffering with the God of the Bible.

Templeton states:
"Why does God's grand design require creatures with teeth designed to crush spines or rend flesh, claws fashioned to seize and tear, venom to paralyze, mouths to suck blood, coils to constrict and smother—even expandable jaws so that prey may be swallowed whole and alive?"... Nature is in Tennyson's vivid phrase, 'red in tooth and claw,' and life is a carnival of blood."

Templeton then concludes: "How could a loving and omnipotent God create such horrors as we have been contemplating?"

One can fully understand his dilemma considering he was indoctrinated to believe the earth was billions of years old. Since the fossil record would therefore represent billions of years of earth history, he would have to believe that the same death, disease, and suffering in the world around us has been going on for millions and millions of years and cannot be the result of sin, the Fall and the Curse.

One wonders whether Templeton would ever have written his Farewell to God, had the church in his day rejected the millions of years, shown the fallibility of the dating methods, and taught creation...

Evangelist Will Building of Ha...

CULTURE IN CRISIS

GRAFFITI ALLEY

The hopelessness and lack of meaning in life, as expressed within this alley, represent what happens when the Bible (our only absolute authority) is taken out of a culture, as has happened in once-Christian nations.

CHARLES TEMPLETON EXHIBIT

This exhibit brings to life a sad example of what can happen when the church tolerates the teaching of millions of years and evolution. Charles Templeton, once a popular evangelist alongside Billy Graham, abandoned Christianity and wrote a book called *Farewell to God*. His situation has been repeated millions of times by young people who are brought up in a church that accepts ideas about millions of years and evolution, unaware it erodes the very foundation of faith.

If the foundations are destroyed, What can the righteous do?
—PSALM 11:3

CULTURE IN CRISIS ROOM

This room shows where the problem in the culture began. A church whose leadership has accepted contemporary ideas about millions of years and evolution is featured. The pastor is preaching that Christians can reinterpret Genesis to fit with man's ideas about the age of the earth. The adults are listening, but the teenage children are not. They see the hypocrisy of such a position that undermines biblical authority. This attack on biblical authority is represented by the wrecking ball smashing into the foundation of the church.

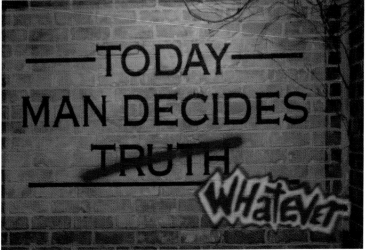

The same church family seen in the broken window of the church, are seen in the privacy of their home. The teens are really no different from the other youth in their culture today — the girl is on the phone discussing a possible abortion, and the boys are shooting up drugs and looking at pornographic websites.

When Christians and Christian families no longer promote the absolute authority of God's Word, they reap the consequences in the next generation.

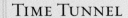

TIME TUNNEL

What is the solution to this distressing culture with so many families in crisis? How did all this happen? Walk thru the corridor of the Time Tunnel, and go back to the beginning of biblical history to find these important answers.

SIX DAYS THEATER

This wide-screen spectacular video presentation summarizes the six days of creation, as recorded in Chapter 1 of Genesis, with an overview of the sequence of events in the Creation Week. God's perfect creation of our world and the universe is revealed.

This dramatic presentation prepares people for the Wonders Room — where they will witness the incredible design of God's creation — and the first of the Seven C's as they begin their walk through the true history of the world.

And God said,
Let the earth bring forth grass,

the herb yielding seed,

and the fruit tree yielding fruit
after its kind,

SIX DAYS THEATER

WONDERS ROOM

WONDERS ROOM

The first verse of the Bible begins, "In the beginning God created . . . ." This room scientifically confirms this verse in a breathtaking presentation.

Fifteen videos, shown one after the other on monitors around the room, leaves viewers with evidence of the only explanation that makes sense — there has to be a powerful Intelligence behind the universe. These videos loosely follow the six-day sequence of creation, from the creation of light and the universe (Day 1) to humans (Day 6), enhancing a beautiful room filled with bright and majestic images of our world.

On the standing exhibit, a verse from the first chapter, verse 20 in the book of Romans states that the Creator is so obvious that everyone is without excuse if they don't believe. The rapid-fire images on the monitor under the verse remind us of the Creator's obvious handiwork.

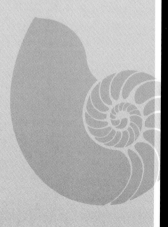

CREATURES of the SEA

THE SUPREME GOD

THE EVERLASTING GOD

THE GOD OF TRUTH

I AM

THE HOLY GOD

GOD ALMIGHTY

THE GOD OF GLORY

IN THE BEGINNING, GOD...

THE RIGHTEOUS GOD

THE LIVING GOD

THE GOOD LORD

JEHOVAH

I AM

GOD WITH US

SAVIOR

REDEEMER

JUDGE

The Wonders Room not only makes it obvious there is a God, but also tells us who this God is — the Creator God of the Bible — as revealed by the names in the room as visitors pass through this unforgettable room.

For the invisible things of *God* from the *Creation* of the world *Clearly Seen*

For since the creation of the world His invisible attributes are clearly seen, being understood by the things that are made, even His eternal power and Godhead, so that they are without excuse,

— ROMANS 1:20

MADE to SERVE the CREATOR

CREATION

ADAM NAMING THE ANIMALS

As people walk through the lush Garden of Eden, visitors learn how Adam could name so many animals in a single day. Experience the beauty of creation as you see the dinosaurs living alongside Adam and Eve. Yes, dinosaurs lived with people — they didn't die out millions of years before people appeared.

Creation Walk, the 7 C's of creation

Now begins the centerpiece of the Creation Museum — a walk through the history of the world as recorded in the Bible, based on the concept of 7 C's — or the seven major periods of history: Creation, Corruption, Catastrophe, Confusion, Christ, Cross, and Consummation

This journey through history is a multimedia adventure — incorporating the latest in cutting-edge technology to communicate effectively on multiple levels, a memorable presentation visitors of any age will enjoy. Most importantly, this 7 C's walk connects the Bible to the real world and answers skeptical questions of the age.

From informative audio to realistic sound effects, visitors can view a variety of video presentations and numerous displays, which explain the exhibits in more detail while answering the most common questions about science, theology, and the Bible.

Even kids will experience the history of the world simply by viewing the exhibits, such as Adam and Eve, dinosaurs, animatronics, human figures, Noah's ark, dioramas, etc. The animals are all peaceful and vegetarian in the Garden (but that will change after mankind's sin).

With the beauty and perfection of God's creation surrounding visitors, they prepare to see how God's perfect plan was destroyed through sin, and how His love is revealed in His plan for mankind's salvation.

CREATION OF EVE

The first woman, Eve, made from Adam's side. This real event was the first marriage and shows God's plan for the family today.

Out of the ground the LORD God caused to grow every tree that is pleasing to the sight and good for food; the tree of life also in the midst of the garden...

THE TREE OF LIFE

The tree stands with limbs outstretched in the heart of the exquisite Garden of Eden. Stunningly detailed, over 31,000 leaves were each placed by hand upon the tree during its construction. Twenty-five feet tall and fifty feet wide at the top, the Tree of Life represents the essence of what was lost with Adam and Eve's fateful decision to sin, and a reminder to mankind of God's promise of salvation.

And the LORD God commanded the man, saying, "Of every tree of the garden you may freely eat; "but of the tree of the knowledge of good and evil you shall not eat, for in the day that you eat of it you shall surely die."

—GENESIS 2:16-17

The Creation Museum depicts pre-Fall animals as vegetarians, reflecting the "very good" creation that did not include suffering and death.

GOD'S FIRST COMMANDMENT

Adam and Even enjoy a swim in the pool by the waterfall, while the serpent plots overhead. The saddest day in the history of the universe, which affected all of creation, is about to occur.

A FALLEN WORLD

Adam and Eve's disobedience of God's first command would lead to a world spiraling into corruption, death, disease, and suffering.

NOW the serpent was more cunning than any beast of the field which the LORD God had made. And he said to the woman, "Has God indeed said, 'You shall not eat of every tree of the garden'?"

—GENESIS 3:1

CORRUPTION

THE CAVE OF SORROWS

People experience some of the horrible results caused by mankind's sin. These horrors aren't God's fault, but our fault, because we sinned against a holy God. Because of sin, we are separated from God and will be forever, but there is a solution to these terrible things and to our separation from God.

THE SACRIFICE SCENE

God's plan for this now-fallen creation and our sin is revealed. This historical sacrifice of a perfect lamb is a foreshadowing of the sacrifice of Christ.

Therefore, just as
through one man sin
entered the world, and
death through sin, and thus
death spread to all men,
because all sinned.
—ROMANS 5:12

Death would not only be revealed in nature, as exemplified by Cain standing over his brother's lifeless body. The world's first murder — Cain killing Abel — culminates the terrible effects of mankind's sin.

CORRUPTION VALLEY

The numerous effects of sin are clearly illustrated in this exhibit. The lush beauty and peace of the Garden of Eden is gone forever. Adam now must work hard in the fields for his food, toiling against weeds, thorns, and thistles. An animatronic dinosaur eats a fresh kill (animals are no longer vegetarian, as they were in the Garden). Death is now a daily part of life on this fallen world.

Many of the most popular questions about the origin of death and disease are also answered. Seeking answers beyond the issue of death and suffering? Want to know who was Cain's wife? Visitors learn the answer as they walk into Methuselah's tent.

Catastrophe looms ahead for mankind, but key historical figures like Methuselah and Noah play an important part in God's amazing plan.

METHUSELAH'S TENT

An animatronic Methuselah, 969 years old, explains what happened to Adam's descendants and warns about what's coming in the next C of the 7 C's of history. Methuselah lived during the lifetimes of both Adam and Noah, and provides a pivotal link and source of history that is passed down to Noah so the story of creation, and the pre-Flood history of man, would survive the coming catastrophe.

God keeps His Promises

THIS is the book of the genealogy of ADAM. In the day that God created man, He made him in the likeness of God. He created them male and female, and blessed them and called them Mankind in the day they were created. And Adam lived one hundred and thirty years, and begot a son in his own likeness, after his image, and named him Seth. After he begot Seth, the days of Adam were eight hundred years; and he had sons and daughters. So all the days that Adam lived were nine hundred and thirty years; and he died. Seth lived one hundred and five years, and begot Enosh. After he begot Enosh, Seth lived eight hundred and seven years, and had sons and daughters. So all the days of Seth were nine hundred and twelve years; and he died. Enosh lived ninety years, and begot Cainan. After he begot Cainan, Enosh lived eight hundred and fifteen years, and had sons and daughters. So all the days of Enosh were nine hundred and five years; and he died. Cainan lived seventy years, and begot Mahalalel. After he begot Mahalalel, Cainan lived eight hundred and forty years, and had sons and daughters. So all the days of Cainan were nine hundred and ten years; and he died. Mahalalel lived sixty-five years, and begot Jared. After he begot Jared, Mahalalel lived eight hundred and thirty years, and had sons and daughters. So all the days of Mahalalel were eight hundred and ninety-five years; and he died. Jared lived one hundred and sixty-two years, and begot Enoch. After he begot Enoch, Jared lived eight hundred years, and had sons and daughters. So all the days of Jared were nine hundred and sixty-two years; and he died. Enoch lived sixty-five years, and begot Methuselah. After he begot Methuselah, Enoch walked with God three hundred years, and had sons and daughters. So all the days of Enoch were three hundred and sixty-five years. And Enoch walked with God; and he was not, for God took him. Methuselah lived one hundred and eighty-seven years, and begot Lamech. After he begot Lamech, Methuselah lived seven hundred and eighty-two years, and had sons and daughters. So all the days of METHUSELAH were nine hundred and sixty-nine years; and he died. Lamech lived one hundred and eighty-two years, and had a son. And he called his name NOAH, saying, "This one will comfort us concerning our work and the toil of our hands, because of the ground which the LORD has cursed." After he begot Noah, Lamech lived five hundred and ninety-five years, and had sons and daughters. So all the days of Lamech were seven hundred and seventy-seven years; and he died. And Noah was five hundred years old, and Noah begot Shem, Ham, and Japheth.

—GENESIS 5

Methuselah

The oldest man on record is Methuselah. He was born two centuries before Adam died, and he lived long enough to see his grandson Noah build the Ark. He died just before the Flood, at the ripe old age of 969.

 # CATASTROPHE

This full-scale cross-section of the ark represents only one percent of the actual ark, but does reveal in exquisite detail the types of construction techniques, tools, and skills needed to construct a vessel using God's specifications that could survive a worldwide flood.

As people climb the ramp into the ark section, they will hear a scoffer mocking Noah, refusing to believe the world was soon to be destroyed.

Also be amazed at details that a master craftsman put into Noah's workbench, including cubits for measurement.

NOAH AND HIS FOREMAN: In a workroom complete with plans and models, Noah stands gazing up at the ark under construction. The workroom has examples of early tools — the types of tools that might have been used in the time Noah lived.

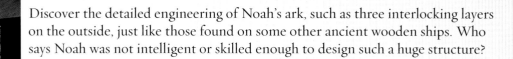

Discover the detailed engineering of Noah's ark, such as three interlocking layers on the outside, just like those found on some other ancient wooden ships. Who says Noah was not intelligent or skilled enough to design such a huge structure?

As visitors walk inside the ark—they see another animatronic figure building inside the ark.

Noah was a just man, perfect in his generations. Noah walked with God.
— Genesis 6:9

THE VOYAGE ROOM

Information about the ark and its cargo as well as answers to many questions about how Noah and his family solved the problems of looking after all the animal kinds in such a large vessel are revealed throughout the exhibits within the Voyage Room. They detail possible solutions for storage, feeding and caring for the animals, as well as giving an idea of scale. From the ark's initial hours of the catastrophic journey through to its safe arrival on land, the Voyage Room takes an important and realistic look at this historic journey.

Near the exit of the Voyage Room, the Rainbow Covenant exhibit reminds visitors of God's enduring promise.

"I set My rainbow in the cloud, and it shall be for the sign of the covenant between Me and the earth."
— GENESIS 9:13

FLOOD GEOLOGY ROOM

The Catastrophe Begins

As the floodwaters covered the earth and then receded, the face of the earth was reshaped into the landscape and formations seen today. From the fossils to the mountains and continents which formed, the earth still bears the marks of the biblical flood. Numerous videos, detailed signs, a breathtaking mural, and dioramas of Mount St. Helens and Grand Canyon located within the museum's Flood Geology Room explain many of the evidences concerning the global flood of Noah's day (from geology, paleontology, and biology). The Catastrophe phase of the 7 C's journey is explored in depth in easy to understand displays.

...on that day all the fountains of the great deep were broken up, and the windows of heaven were opened.
— GENESIS 7:11

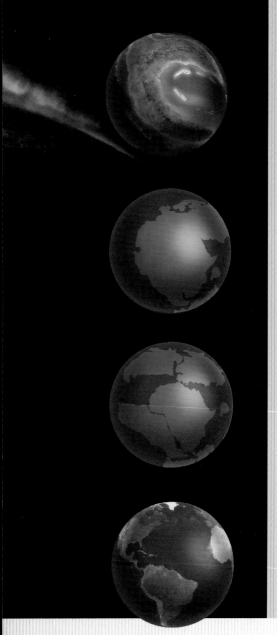

The Flood Geology Room is set up to take you through the Flood chronologically, from the initiation of the Flood, the Flood itself, and the events after the Flood (such as the Ice Age and the spread of animals around the world).

Guest are introduced to Catastrophic Plate Tectonics as one model that explains the breakup of the original continent and the source of much of the floodwaters.

The flood rearranges the earth

God's World and God's Word agree

The origin of people groups, including information about skin color, language, families, etc. are explored in this section of the Creation Museum. All to point out an important biblical truth: all humans belong to just one race – the human race.

CONFUSION

The next stop in this journey of biblical history is Confusion. The biblical story of Babel is not only a tale of man's foolish pride and disobedience to God; it is also a historical event which explains much of the world as it exists today in terms of different people groups and different cultures.

The Tower of Babel occurred a century or two after the global Flood. Assyrian-styled winged bull statues flank a water exhibit, framing a visually-stunning video program, summarizing the events at the Tower of Babel. This event resulted in the separation of the human gene pool and the beginning of cultural differences for mankind — such as language and specialized skills among regions of the earth.

Vital teaching is also given concerning God's covenant with Abraham, where He spelled out the promise of a Messiah (God first mentioned this Promised One at the sacrifice scene after the Cave of Sorrows).

The caveman exhibit also shows that cavemen were not primitive— just real humans who lived in caves which provided natural shelter!

THE HUMAN RACE

All culturally unique, yet all still belonging to only one race, the human race. The event of the Tower of Babel scattered people over the earth resulting in isolated groups, each with distinct characteristics, as shown in these photos. Such differences resulting from the enormous created variability of the human gene pool are only surface differences. The major differences among the different people groups are simply cultural.

> So the Lord scattered them abroad from there upon the face of all the earth; and they left off building the city.
>
> — GENESIS 11:8

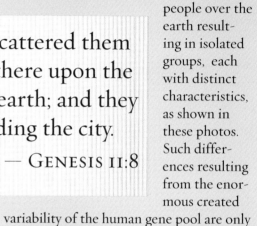

As people groups settled throughout the earth, conquering their environments, and developing new skills, one thing remained the same. They were still sinners in a fallen world. But on the next stage of the 7C's journey, God's answer for mankind's redemption would be revealed.

Babel Explains Our Differences

AND THE
WORD
BECAME
FLESH
AND DWELT
AMONG US,
AND WE
BEHELD
HIS GLORY...
JOHN 1:14

CHRIST

The climax of the Creation Museum is focused on mankind's Savior, Jesus Christ. God created the world knowing that it would serve as the stage for the gospel message: the prophets promised that the Messiah was coming to pay the penalty for mankind's sin and offer a free gift of salvation, a way to end the separation from God created at the Fall of Man.

THE LAST ADAM THEATER

A powerful presentation of the gospel, unlike anything you've seen elsewhere, explains what the Creation Museum is all about — sharing the truth of creation, the fall of man and its effects, and reminding people of the salvation which God has made available to everyone. The three-screen, high-quality presentation runs every 20 minutes, and serves as an important link in understanding the real meaning and importance of Genesis history to Christ's sacrifice of Himself on the Cross.

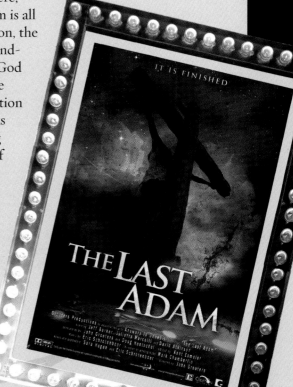

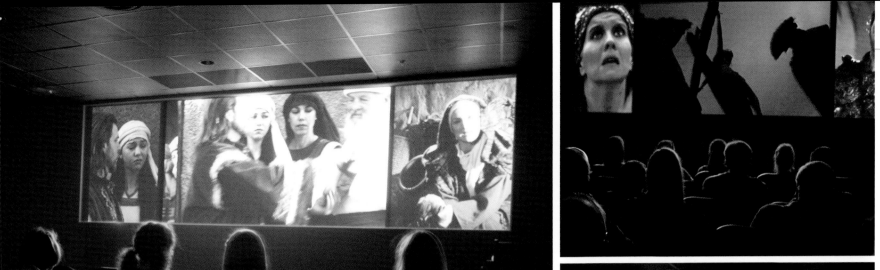

CONSUMMATION
THE FULFILLMENT OF GOD'S WORD

One day the Creator will remake His creation.
He will cast out death and the disobedient, and
dwell eternally with all those who trust in Him.
Earth will be restored to a perfect place—
as it was before sin.

Death and hell were cast into the lake of fire. . . .
And I saw a new heaven and a new earth.
Revelation 20:14–21:1

CROSS
THE ANSWER OF GOD'S WORD

The penalty for mankind's disobedience was death.
Jesus, the Messiah, died on a cross to pay
that penalty. He rose from the dead, providing
life for all who trust in Him.

Christ has once suffered for sins, the just for the unjust.
1 Peter 3:18

CHRIST
THE PROMISE OF GOD'S WORD

The Creator became a man, our relative—
a member of the human race. His name was
Jesus of Nazareth, who obeyed God in
everything, unlike the first man, Adam.

When the fullness of the time was come,
God sent forth his Son, made of a woman.
Galatians 4:4

...if you confess with your mouth the Lord
Jesus and believe in your heart that God has
raised Him from the dead, you will be saved.
— ROMANS 10:9

The three C's room leading up to the Last Adam Theater
represents the heart of the ministry of Answers in Genesis
— to present the gospel of Jesus Christ to all.

CROSS

The Creation Museum includes a chapel built to represent a first-century synagogue, similar to the ones where Jesus Christ preached about God's plan for His creation. Museum guests are encouraged to take a moment in the peace of the chapel to reflect upon the biblical history and message of salvation they have just seen revealed.

CONSUMMATION

One day, at the consummation, the Creator will remake His creation. He will cast out death and the disobedient, and dwell eternally with those who trust in Him. What a wonderful future God has planned for those who love Him!

"And God will wipe away every tear from their eyes; there shall be no more death, nor sorrow, nor crying. There shall be no more pain, for the former things have passed away." Then He who sat on the throne said, "Behold, I make all things new."

—REVELATION 21:4-5

LEAVING A LEGACY

The Creation Museum is really the legacy of Ken Ham's godly parents who trained their children to stand uncompromisingly on the authority of the Word of God. A special exhibit in the wall of the chapel outside the Last Adam Theater (consisting of a photograph of Ken Ham's parents, his father's Bible and a small Noah's ark model Ken's father built for him) challenges each visitor as to what legacy they are leaving in this world to others (children, close relatives, friends etc).

PALM PLAZA

PALM PLAZA

Lined with interesting exhibits of fossils and more, Palm Plaza is designed with an Egyptian architectural influence. The plaza is a location where visitors can select refreshments, and it also contains the museum's unique collection of dinosaur stamps from around the world.

DRAGON LEGENDS THEATRE

This fascinating eleven minute video was filmed at a magnificent castle in England. The topic of the theater's "Dragons and Dinosaurs" video challenges museum guests with the possibility what were called dragons, may have been what we refer to today as dinosaurs. Discover more about dragon legends from around the world, and information that may help you to see these amazing "legendary" creatures in a whole new light.

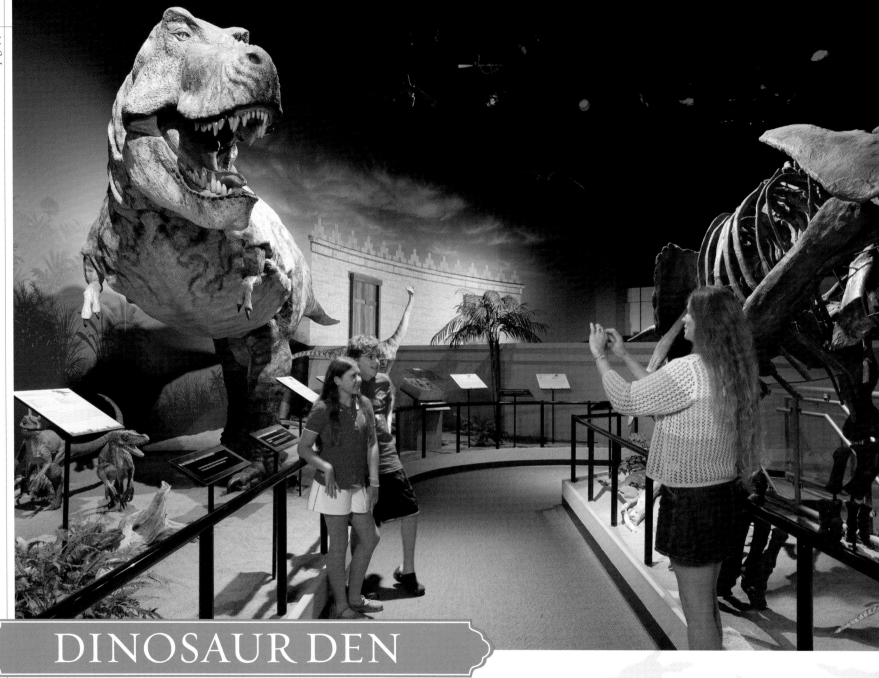

DINOSAUR DEN

Biblical history is the key to understanding dinosaurs!

DINOSAUR EXHIBIT

An arched doorway leads into a two-story, life-sized dinosaur exhibit. Signs take guests chronologically through a biblical explanation of dinosaurs, and the dinosaur models are guaranteed to fascinate everyone! From dinosaur eggs, to the skeleton of a triceratops, to the massive *T. rex* looming large above visitors, it's a great area for a family photo and an important perspective on seeing dinosaurs not as products of millions of years, but as part of a created world only thousands of years old.

DINOSAURS GALORE

A favorite destination for visitors, Dinosaur Den is home to 16 different dinosaurs, and a triceratops skeleton. There are over 29 dinosaurs in the Creation Museum, five of which are animatronic. Some estimate that there may have been as many as 55 kinds of dinosaurs represented on the ark during the global flood.

Visitors can stand face to
face with some of God's most
amazing creations. Popular
dinosaurs and unique
creatures are hallmarks of
this world class exhibit.

CHASMOSAURUS

ARCHAEOPTERYX

PROTOCERATOPS

TRICERATOPS

ANUROGNATHUS

"Look now at the behemoth, which I made along with you; He eats grass like an ox. See now, his strength is in his hips, And his power is in his stomach muscles. He moves his tail like a cedar; The sinews of his thighs are tightly knit. His bones are like beams of bronze, His ribs like bars of iron."

— JOB 40:15-18

CERATOSAURUS

EDAPHESAURUS

ORNITHOLESTES

VELOCIRAPTOR

BONES BROUGHT TO LIFE

Sculptures by paleoartist Buddy Davis as well as real fossils and casts feature in this one-of-a-kind dinosaur exhibit. While some aspects of the dinosaurs remain a mystery — such as color and behavior, explorers throughout world continue to discover new and exciting variations of these animals created with others during the six-day creation week.

Fossilized clutch of segnosaur dinosaur eggs.

DRAGON HALL BOOKSTORE

SAINT GEORGE AND THE DRAGON

The image of Saint George's battle with a "dragon" decorates one wall of the Dragon Hall Bookstore. Legend states that strong of faith and therefore fearless, he battled the beast to save a king's daughter, and then offered to kill the beast if the townspeople would convert to Christianity — which legend also says they did.

DRAGON HALL GIFT AND BOOKSTORE

An animatronic *Pteranodon* stands guard above the entrance to the museum's bookstore! Themed after a medieval castle's great hall and complete with dragon sculptures and stained glass windows depicting dragon legends, guests are reminded once again that the dragons legends possibly could have been dinosaurs.

DRAGON HALL
BOOKSTORE

Noah's Café

Museum visitors relax in a pleasant Noah's ark-themed environment, and enjoy quality food at very reasonable prices. Sandwiches or daily hot entreés, grilled food, hot dogs, ice cream, and more are served. Other dining options at the Creation Museum include the Lakeside Grill, looking out over the beautifully-landscaped grounds, the Plaza Café or the Burrito Bar, both located in the Palm Plaza.

NOAH'S CAFE

NATURE TRAILS

The grounds surrounding the Creation Museum are unique living exhibits that continue to glorify God through His many creations. A visit to the Botanical Gardens is a must during a museum visit. Guests can see the carnivorous bog garden, the rainforest area, the butterfly and hummingbird garden, waterfalls, a swinging bridge, and more as they experience God's handiwork all around them.

Visitors stroll through the Carnivorous Bog Garden, complete with fog system, river birches, weeping junipers, and thousands of perennials, bog plants, and carnivorous plants.

Photo opportunities are abundant as guests wind their way through the nature trails with lush plants in bloom, and the sound of soothing water features located throughout the grounds.

O LORD, our Lord, how majestic is your name in all the earth! You have set your glory above the heavens.

— PSALM 8:1

More than 550 varieties of plants greet visitors in the gardens and provide a wonderful setting to behold God's creativity.

"In the beginning was the Word, and the Word was with God, and the Word was God. He was in the beginning with God. All things were made through Him, and without Him nothing was made that was made."

—John 1:1-3

Bridges, topiaries, pavilions, waterfalls, a pergola, a gazebo, and wildlife each provide a unique perspective on God's amazing creation.

A *T. rex* topiary invites guests to cross the swinging bridge, and stands ready to delight the youngest of visitors!

A visit to the Creation Museum isn't complete without a stop at the petting zoo! Not only is the petting zoo a fun place for children and adults to experience close up encounters with unique animals, as with other aspects of the Creation Museum experience, there is an opportunity to learn. Not only can the petting zoo develop a respect and appreciation for God's animal creations, it can also help answer important questions related to the history of Noah's ark.

The opening of the museum's petting zoo represents an important effort to make the museum not only a fun but educational facility for children of every age, all while honoring biblical history and the truth of God's Word.

Whether touring the dinosaur exhibit or making friends with the zonkey, the Creation Museum is an unforgettable destination for families!

PETTING ZOO

The zonkey (at right), the Zorse (top left), and donkeys all belong to the horse kind. This helps people understand there can be great variation within each kind of animal God created. And it was animal kinds that Noah took aboard the ark — a dog kind, a cat kind, a horse kind, etc.

Then God said, "Let the earth bring forth the living creature according to its kind: cattle and creeping thing and beast of the earth, each according to its kind"; and it was so.

—GENESIS 1:24

The mischievous animals enjoy the attention of museum visitors — as well as some good old-fashioned fun among themselves!

Curly Sue

Did you know that llamas are members of the camel kind?

Of the birds after their kind, of animals after their kind, and of every creeping thing of the earth after its kind, two of every kind will come to you to keep them alive.

—GENESIS 6:20

Did you know that sheep and goats are all part of one animal kind? Other petting zoo residents include bunnies and turkeys. Whether feeding the animals, petting them, or simply having fun watching them, the petting zoo is a delightful way to complete a young person's Creation Museum experience!

CREATION MUSEUM

Prepare to believe.

AN ANNUAL DESTINATION

The Creation Museum continues to expand and offer new programs and exhibits throughout the year. The museum grounds change as well with each season — from the deep colors of autumn to spring's abundance of blossoms. Visitors are encouraged to return and bring family and friends as their guests for an unforgettable journey of discovery. Conveniently located, a trip to the Creation Museum is faith-affirming, and will be an experience your family will treasure. For more information on museum events and activities, please visit www.creationmuseum.org .

Photo Credits

L = left, TL = top left, BL = bottom left, C = center, CR = center right,
CL = Center left, R = right, TR = top right, BR = bottom right

DeCesare, Paul: pg. 85-B

Dudley, Tim: pg. 9, pg. 11, pg 13-TL, pg. 22-BC, pg. 24, pg. 25-TL, pg. 35-BR, pg. 48-49-TC, pg. 57-BR, pg. 70, pg. 73-BR

Jolly, Lynn: pg. 48-door, pg. 80, pg. 81-TL, 85-TL, pg. 86-TL, B, pg. 87-BR, pg. 89-TR, pg. 92-TR, BR, pg. 93-L, BR, pg. 94, pg. 95-BR, TL

Lewis, Daniel: pg. 3, pg. 69-TL, pg. 77-TR, pg. 84, pg. 88-L, pg. 89-TL, BL, CR

Minnard, Deb: pg. 7-TR, BR, pg. 8, pg. 17-T, pg. 19, pg. 50, pg. 69-BL, pg. 73-TR, pg. 85-BR, pg. 87-T, pg. 89-T, BL, pg. 90-L, pg. 91-B, pg. 92-L, pg. 93-TR, pg. 95-BL, C, TR, Back Cover-T

Minnard, Marty: pg. 6, pg. 14-T, pg. 82-BL, Back Cover-B

Rockafellow, Dan: pg. 12, pg 13-R, pg. 14-BR, pg. 15, pg. 16, pg. 18-TL, pg. 18-BL, pg. 18-R, pg. 20, pg. 21-T, B, pg 22-L, TR, CR, pg. 23, pg. 26, pg. 28-BL, pg 28-29, pg 29-B, pg. 31-L, CT, RT, BL, pg. 32-TL, BL, R, pg. 33-L, TR, pg. 34, pg. 35-TL, CR, pg. 36-TL, TR, pg. 37, pg. 38, pg. 39-TR, pg. 41, pg. 42, pg. 43-T, pg. 44, pg.45-L, R, pg. 46, pg. 47-B, pg. 48-BL, BR, pg. 49-BR, pg. 51-BL, R, pg. 53, pg. 54-TL, pg. 55, pg. 58-BL, TL, pg. 59-BR, pg. 60, pg. 61-all, pg. 64, pg. 65-R, pg. 69-TR, CR, BR, pg. 71, pg. 72, pg. 74, pg. 75-all, pg. 76-all, pg. 77-L, pg. 78, pg. 79-TL, TR, pg. 81-BL, R, pg. 82-TL, pg. 83, All Front Cover Images

Welch, Laura: pg. 13-BL, pg. 25-BL, R, pg. 30, pg 31-BR, pg. 35-BL, pg. 43-BR, pg. 47-TL, TR, pg. 49-R, pg. 52-BL, pg. 54-BL, BR, pg. 56-B, pg. 65-BL, pg. 68-L, pg. 79-CL, BL, pg. 96

Murals & Illustrations

Coe, Mark: pg. 63-TR, CR

Einselen, Jon: pg. 17-B, pg. 58-B, pg. 62

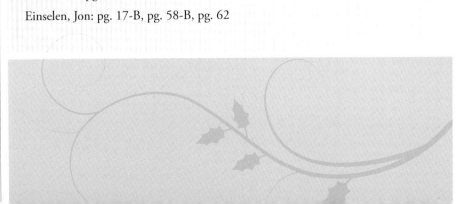